Leonardo da Vinci
1452-1519

Leonardo da Vinci (1452-1519) was born in Italy, the son of a gentleman of Florence. He made significant contributions to many different disciplines, including anatomy, botany, geology, astronomy, architecture, paleontology, and cartography.

He is one of the greatest and most influential painters of all time, creating masterpieces such as the *Mona Lisa* and *The Last Supper*. And his imagination led him to create designs for things such as an armored car, scuba gear, a parachute, a revolving bridge, and flying machines. Many of these ideas were so far ahead of their time that they weren't built until centuries later.

He is the original "Renaissance Man" whose genius extended to all five areas of today's STEAM curriculum: Science, Technology, Engineering, the Arts, and Mathematics.

You can find more information on Leonardo da Vinci in *Who Was Leonardo da Vinci?* by Roberta Edwards (Grosset & Dunlap, 2005), *Magic Tree House Fact Tracker: Leonardo da Vinci* by Mary Pope Osborne and Natalie Pope Bryce (Random House, 2009), and *Leonardo da Vinci for Kids: His Life and Ideas* by Janis Herbert (Chicago Review Press, 1998).

LITTLE LEONARDO'S™

Fascinating World
of PALEONTOLOGY

Illustrated by
GREG PAPROCKI

Written by
JEFF BOND

GIBBS SMITH
TO ENRICH AND INSPIRE HUMANKIND

PALEONTOLOGY is the science of studying FOSSILS. A fossil is any trace of life from the distant past. Studying fossils is almost like traveling through time.

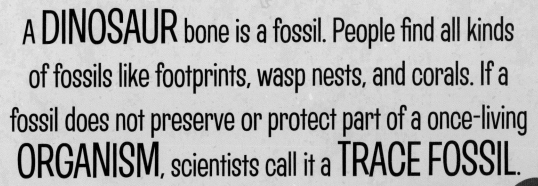

A DINOSAUR bone is a fossil. People find all kinds of fossils like footprints, wasp nests, and corals. If a fossil does not preserve or protect part of a once-living ORGANISM, scientists call it a TRACE FOSSIL.

Fossils can preserve life forms that have since gone EXTINCT, such as a DIPLODOCUS.

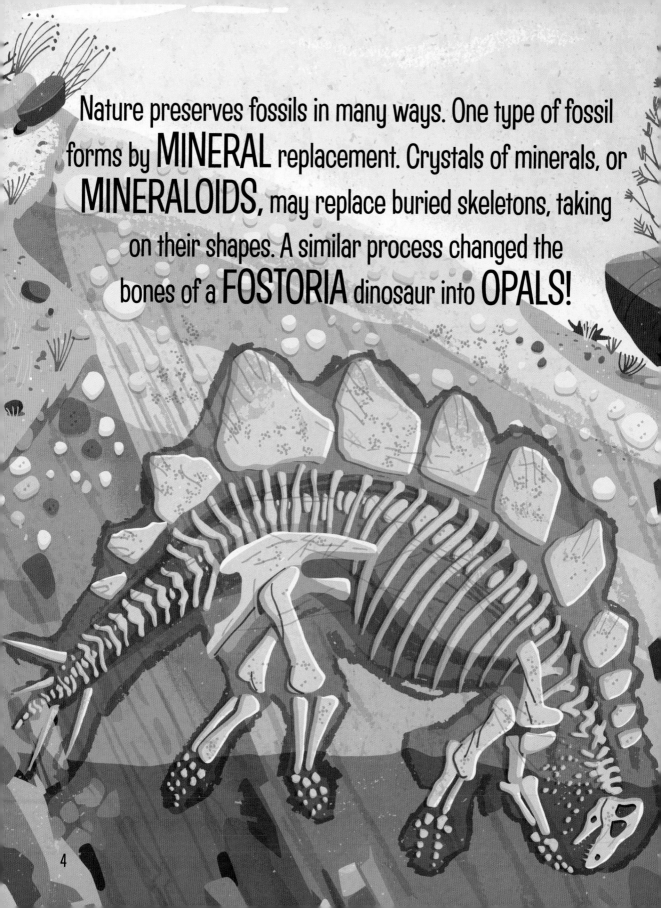

Nature preserves fossils in many ways. One type of fossil forms by MINERAL replacement. Crystals of minerals, or MINERALOIDS, may replace buried skeletons, taking on their shapes. A similar process changed the bones of a FOSTORIA dinosaur into OPALS!

More often, dinosaur bones, and even PETRIFIED WOOD, become fossils in a different way. Bones and wood act like sponges.

They filter minerals out of ground water, and then these minerals start to grow crystals.

These crystals fill up the fossil, protecting it for AGES.

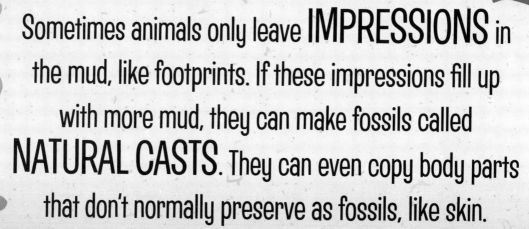

Sometimes animals only leave IMPRESSIONS in the mud, like footprints. If these impressions fill up with more mud, they can make fossils called NATURAL CASTS. They can even copy body parts that don't normally preserve as fossils, like skin.

Other natural systems can preserve fossils, but they are still pretty rare. Some natural forces, such as EROSION, can also destroy them. Hunting for fossils sometimes feels like a race against time, and fossil LABS have to work quickly and carefully to recover and repair their fossils.

Scientists use many methods to study fossils. One method compares differences in the same bone type from a variety of animals. Small changes in shape lets finger bones form grasping hands, swimming flippers, or flying wings. Patterns of bone shapes help scientists predict what ancient animals could do with their bodies.

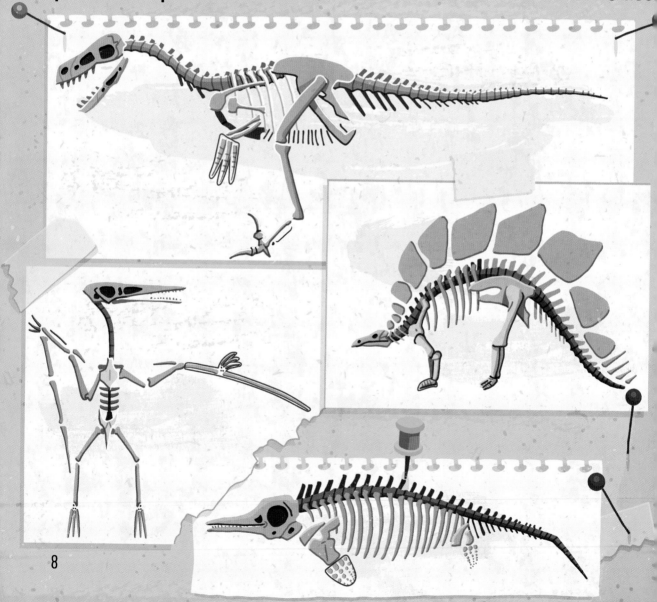

MATRIX is rock that surrounds a fossil. It hides clues from ancient HABITATS. Methods such as SEDIMENTOLOGY reveal how certain rocks form, and these rocks can tell us where rivers used to flow or where deserts covered the land. cientists can use such techniques to explore prehistoric environments.

Figuring out which fossils belong to which SPECIES really challenges scientists. Some living things completely change shape as they age. Scientists call these changes ONTOGENY. For example, a baby PROTOCERATOPS hatched with a head that looked like a parrot's head. As adults, they grew large frills, like a Triceratops.

Together, anatomy, sedimentology, and other techniques work like parts of an imaginary time machine. Scientists can use them to learn about prehistoric life, almost like traveling back in time. What discoveries will you make in the distant past?

PETRIFIED—FOSSILIZING A SPONGE

You can copy the natural processes that make dinosaur bones and petrified wood become as hard as rock. All it takes is a few tools and a few days—even if it feels like millions of years! If you're using hot water, you will need a grown-up's help.

What You Need:

- ¤ A cup or two of water, preferably hot
- ¤ A pot or other container that can withstand heat
- ¤ Water-soluble crystals—salt, borax, or alum work fine
- ¤ A piece of sponge
- ¤ A clear plastic cup

What You Do:

1. Have an adult heat the water to near boiling (this project can also be done with a microwave—whatever makes the water hot should do).

2. Slowly stir in your crystal of choice, adding more a little at a time until only a few grains remain at the bottom of the pot. When the water will no longer dissolve more crystals, allow it to cool.

3. Place your sponge in a clear plastic cup then pour some of the crystal mixture over it.

4. Now the waiting begins. Check on it every day and take note of what new features you can observe as the water dries, or evaporates out of the cup. Once the water completely dries out, pull out the sponge and take a close look. You should be able to see crystals growing inside the sponge, just like a real dinosaur bone.

OPTIONAL: For more fun, try petrifying dinosaur-shaped sponges. You can often find water-soluble capsules with such sponges inside in supermarkets or toy stores.

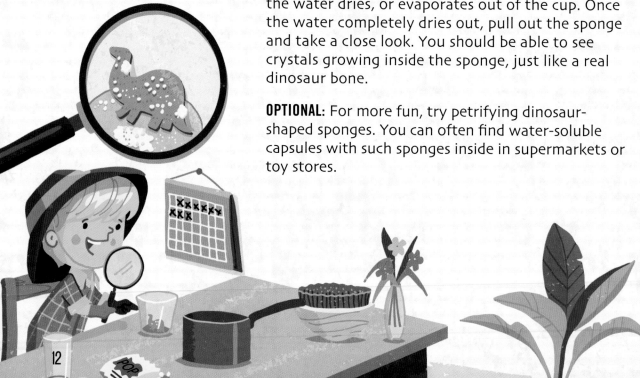

FOSSIL CLONES

Remember how some fossils form as natural copies of the original? Scientists have learned from that process how to create copies of the fossils they find. That way, they have a backup in case something happens to the original. This project is a lot of messy fun, so make sure you prepare for cleanup and use tools that won't be ruined by the project.

What You Need:

- ☒ Disposable table covering
- ☒ Plasticine clay
- ☒ Objects to copy (dinosaur toys, sea shells, leaves, or your fingers)
- ☒ Plaster of Paris
- ☒ Water
- ☒ A mixing bowl
- ☒ Craft sticks or disposable spoons
- ☒ Acrylic paint (optional)
- ☒ Toothpicks

What You Do:

1. Prepare your work area by covering it with the table covering. Plaster can take hours to dry, so you should prepare a place to let it sit undisturbed for a while.

2. Roll the plasticine out with your hands or a rolling pin to about half an inch in thickness and at least a few inches in diameter—it doesn't have to be exact. Then curl up the edges into a bowl shape. Gently press the shell, or whatever you're copying, into the clay at the bottom of the bowl then remove it. Seal up any edges that might leak.

3. Mix up the plaster with the water according to the measurements on the plaster package. Use craft sticks or disposable spoons for stirring. LEAVE NO LUMPS! The consistency of the plaster should be somewhere between instant pudding and peanut butter. You may need to add plaster or water in small amounts to get the consistency right. Work quickly—the plaster will begin to harden. You can also color the plaster by mixing in a small amount of acrylic paint.

4. When the plaster is mixed, spoon or pour it into the plasticine mold. Be careful not to overfill it. Gently tap or shake the mold to remove any air bubbles from the bottom. Allow it to sit for a few hours to harden.

5. Once the plaster turns hard and cool, you can remove the plasticine mold. Some shapes might leave plasticine stuck to the plaster copy, so toothpicks can help remove it. If you like, you can paint the copy at this point.

PAPER ICHNOLOGY

Of course, all you need to make a footprint is some mud and a foot. However, this alternative saves the need for bath time afterward, and it can make a fun greeting card! If you've never done origami before, don't worry . . . this folding pattern is extremely free-form and forgiving.

What You Need:

✶ Square or rectangular paper (preferably brown in color), or aluminum foil

What You Do:

1. If you're using paper with different colors on either side, choose which color you want for the footprint and place the paper with that color facing up. Start by folding the square in half lengthwise. It will look like you are closing a book. Give it a good crease then unfold and flatten.

2. The resulting line on the paper is a guideline. Choose one of the corners facing away from you and fold it toward the middle. This corner will trace the inner edges of the middle toe and its neighboring toe. The folded edge will cross the guideline made in Step 1. There's no guideline for this fold—just eyeball it.

3. Now fold the other corner inward, like a mirror image of the other, to complete the middle toe.

4. Fold in the left and right sides at an angle to complete all three toes. Again, just eyeball these folds.

5. Now fold up the bottom edge to form the heel. Try to line it up with the other flaps to create a continuous outline. If you want a rounder heel, you can shape it with two or three flaps instead.

6. The area surrounding your dinosaur footprint will be an irregular pentagon. If you used a particularly springy paper, you can make the flaps lie flatter by folding each corner of this pentagon behind the other side of the model. The more irregular these folds, the more the piece will look like a natural rock form.

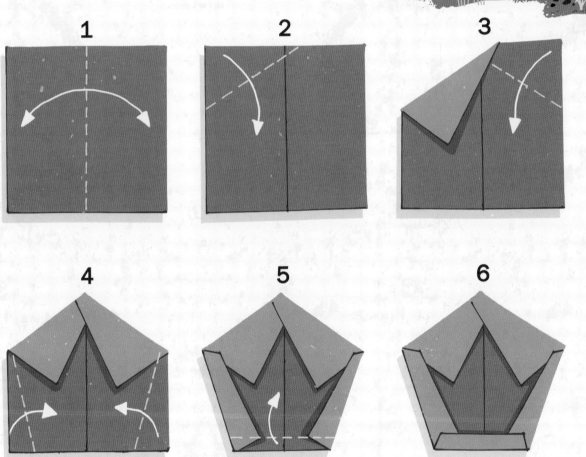

1

2

3

4

5

6

THINK ABOUT THIS: Don't worry if your footprint doesn't look like the picture. Dinosaurs and birds have a wide variety of foot shapes. Your model may just represent a different species. By the way, *ichnology* is the study of footprints. If the feet that made them were stinky, maybe you could call it *ICK-nology*!

15

BUGS IN GUMMY AMBER

Would you ever want to eat a bug? EW! What if you covered it in ten-million-year-old maple syrup? Double EW! Eating bugs in amber would never be a good idea, but you could eat *this* model of amber, if you wanted to. Just don't eat the bug inside! For this project you may need help from a grown-up.

What You Need:

- ✠ Plastic insects small enough to fit completely inside ice tray compartments

- ✠ Ice tray

- ✠ 1/2 cup water or fruit juice (for best results, use 100% juice)

- ✠ Small saucepan

- ✠ Food coloring (optional)

- ✠ 2 tablespoons of gelatin (about 2 packets) or 1/2 tablespoon agar powder

- ✠ 2 tablespoons honey or agave syrup (optional)

- ✠ Turkey baster

What You Do:

1. Rinse the plastic bugs, especially if you intend to make these models as treats. It's best to avoid bug toys with any paint on them. Prepare the ice tray by loading each compartment with at least one bug. Don't let any parts stick out of the tray.

2. Start the gummy mixture by adding water or juice to the pan. If using water, a few drops of food coloring will make better-looking gummy amber. Real amber comes in yellow-orange, orange-red, light green, and pale blue. Apple juice is a great color for amber.

3. Add gelatin to the water and let it soak for a bit. (For a vegetarian option, use agar instead. Agar is a seaweed extract that is sold in whole foods stores or Asian food markets. Agar gummies won't be as firm and won't be transparent.) Heat the mixture over medium heat until all the gelatin or agar is dissolved, stirring continually—do not allow the mixture to boil. It may have the consistency of a thin syrup at this point. Turn off the heat, but keep the mixture on the stove so it doesn't cool too rapidly. If you are using honey or agave syrup, add it now and stir until it dissolves.

4. Use a turkey baster to transfer the gummy mixture to the ice tray. Make sure the mixture completely covers the toy bug. Do not overfill. Depending on the size of the ice tray, it will probably take a few batches of gummy mixture to fill the whole tray. Timing is important for the gelatin/agar to set up, so it's best to work in small batches at a time. Chill the project in the refrigerator for about an hour. The gummies will keep for about a week if kept refrigerated in an airtight container. Again, be careful not to eat the bugs!

EYE-TRAINING GAME

You don't need perfect vision to look for fossils, but you *do* need to know how to see. This game trains your ability to recognize patterns—a vital skill in fossil hunting.

What You Need:

- A collection of about 10–20 small objects, such as dinosaur toys

- One playing partner, at least

- A kitchen timer

- A bag or box large enough to hold at least half the collection

- A blindfold

- A notebook (optional)

- A pencil or pen (optional)

What You Do:

1. **SET:** Roll the collection on a tabletop as if they were dice. If any end up on top of one another or several inches from the group, rearrange them slightly.

2. **BET:** Wager with your partner about the number of objects you think you can find. This number should be no higher than half the collection.

3. **WATCH:** Choose which player goes first. They get one minute to examine the collection (for different challenge levels, vary the time or add it to the wager).

4. **HIDE:** Blindfold the first player. Remove the wagered number of objects and place them in a bag or box out of sight.

5. **SEARCH:** Once the first player removes his/her blindfold, they get one minute to reexamine the collection (this time period can also vary or be added to the wager). They need to identify which objects were removed. Each correct find earns one point. Anything not identified or misidentified counts as a negative point.

6. If you want to treat this as serious training, list in a notebook what wager you made and how you did for each round. Be sure to include all the details of the game: set, bet, watch, hide, search. After a few games, see which element seems hardest then focus on changing that part from game to game. Believe it or not, tracking progress like this is also great training for real science.

7. Repeat the phases of the game for each playing partner. The highest score wins. If you do this as a party game, the collection can make a neat prize!

THINK ABOUT THIS: Try different strategies. Do you remember the objects more easily when you know dinosaur names? Locations? Colors? Shapes? This game can help you learn how you think.

Triceratops ✔
Allosaurus ✔
T-Rex
Stegasaurus ✔
Parasaurolophus
Velociraptor

WHAT YOU SHOULD KNOW: Science cannot work without good observation skills. Without good data, the rest of the process falls apart. This fact proves doubly true for paleontologists: learning how to see helps scientists uncover, repair, and understand fossils.

FIX THE CHOCO-CHIP FOSSILS

Fossil repair takes steady hands, sharp eyes, and a lot of practice! Not many people get to work on irreplaceable fossils, but this project lets you practice the skills without risking the bones.

What You Need:

¤ Chocolate chip cookies

¤ Toothpicks (round, sturdy ones)

¤ Metal forks (optional)

What You Do:

1. The best cookies for this project will have hard chips in a soft cookie. Cheap but fresh store-bought cookies often work best, especially if they have mini M&M's. However, don't be afraid to experiment with different brands.

2. Pretend the chocolate pieces are fossils, and you are a technician in a fossil lab. Just like real fossils, every cookie will present different challenges. Start by observing the cookie and finding where each of the chocolate "fossils" hide. Plan ahead: starting on the edge and working inward will lead to better results.

3. Use a toothpick (preferably) or metal fork to scrape the cookie matrix away from the chocolate. The goal is to remove the chocolate with as little damage as possible. For safety's sake, always scrape away from you or your fingers! You can break the cookie as long as you can control where it cracks.

4. Sometimes working on chunks of cookie away from the fossil leads to better results than doggedly scraping right next to it. Sometimes you can gently pry the fossil out of the cookie without scraping at all. Try finding a cookie that will let you try this! This part of paleontology definitely uses more art than science—sometimes it's all about feeling your way through the project.

WHAT YOU SHOULD KNOW: Chocolate chips may not count as fossils, but the skills used in this project nearly match the ones scientists use to recover and repair real dinosaur bones. Fortunately, cookies are much more forgiving than fossils: breaking a chocolate chip feels much better than breaking an irreplaceable 150-million-year-old fossil! And though you wouldn't want to eat a dinosaur bone, believe it or not, sometimes lab technicians will lick fossil bones! They don't do it to taste them, though, because rock tastes horrible. But bone has a texture that will stick to your tongue, while rock doesn't. It wouldn't be a good idea to try this the next time you visit a museum! Bones on display always have special coatings that help preserve them, so you wouldn't feel the stickiness anyway.

GLOSSARY

AGE (AYJ): Units of geologic time spanning a few million years.

ANATOMY (ah-NAT-oh-mee): The study of body parts and shapes.

DINOSAUR (DIE-no-sore): A diverse group of reptiles that all have a hole in the hip socket. Most of them died out at the end of the Mesozoic era. Birds are the only surviving members of the group, but they are very different from other dinosaurs.

DIPLODOCUS (dih-PLOD-oh-kus): A classic example of the generally long-necked sauropod group of dinosaurs. It had a thin build compared to other sauropods and a whip-like tail tip. It lived in the western US during the Late Jurassic period.

EROSION (ee-ROE-shun): Forces that break rocks down into mud or sand. This can happen with rivers, freezing, or even wind.

EXTINCT (ehk-STINKT): The disappearance of an entire kind or species of living thing. For example, since no more dodo birds remain alive, that species is extinct.

FOSSIL (FAH-suhl): Any trace of life from the distant past. There are no rules on how old something has to be in order to be called a fossil. Old human-made things are known as artifacts, but skeletons or footprints may be called fossils.

FOSTORIA (fah-STORE-ee-ah): A relative of the famous dinosaur Iguanodon that lived in Australia. It was named in 2019.

HABITAT (HAB-ih-tat): Where any plant or animal lives and grows.

IMPRESSION (imp-REH-shun): Marks made by an object pressed into a substance. For example, a shoe pressed into mud will leave behind an impression called a footprint.

LAB (LAB): Short for laboratory, it is a special place for doing science. Labs have to be kept clean and often have unusual tools.

MATRIX (MAY-tricks): Any natural material that surrounds a fossil, like stone, clay, or amber.

MINERAL (MIHN-er-all): A natural crystal not made by a living thing.

MINERALOID (MIHN-er-all-oyd): Rocklike things with some but not all mineral features. For example, obsidian is made from silicon dioxide like quartz, but it does not form crystals.

NATURAL CAST (NACH-er-ull CAST): A naturally made copy of a shape.

ONTOGENY (ahn-TAH-jen-ee): How a body changes as it ages. Caterpillars becoming butterflies is an example of ontogeny.

OPAL (OH-pull): A mineraloid made up of silicon dioxide (like glass) and water. It often forms tiny balls that reflect light in rainbow colors.

ORGANISM (ORE-gun-is-um): A living thing—an individual animal, plant, or single-celled life form.

PALEONTOLOGY (PALE-ee-ahn-TAHL-uh-jee): The scientific study of fossils.

PETRIFIED WOOD (PET-rih-fide WOOD): Wood preserved by tiny crystals that have grown inside it.

PROTOCERATOPS (PRO-toh-SEHR-a-tops): A sheep-sized horned dinosaur from Mongolia. It looked like a Triceratops, but it lacked large horns. Scientists discovered it in 1923.

SEDIMENTOLOGY (SEHD-ih-mehnt-AHL-uh-jee): The study of rocks formed by muds, silts, and sands made by wearing down other kinds of rocks.

SPECIES (SPEE-seez): A type of thing, usually a living thing.

TRACE FOSSIL (TRAYSS FAH-suhl): A type of fossil that tells something about an organism without including any of its parts. Trace fossils may include footprints, nests, eggs, or body impressions.

FRAGILE

Manufactured in China in December 2020 by Crash Paper

First Edition
25 24 23 22 21   5 4 3 2 1

Text © 2021 Gibbs Smith, Publisher
Illustrations © 2021 Greg Paprocki
Little Leonardo™ is a trademark of Gibbs Smith, Publisher.

Published by
Gibbs Smith
P.O. Box 667
Layton, Utah 84041
1.800.835.4993 orders
www.gibbs-smith.com

Designed by Greg Paprocki

Gibbs Smith books are printed on either recycled, 100% post-consumer
waste, FSC-certified papers or on paper produced from sustainable
PEFC-certified forest/controlled wood source. Learn
more at www.pefc.org.

Library of Congress Control Number: 2020942768
ISBN: 978-1-4236-5715-6

Some paleontologists of note...

Georges Cuvier (1769–1832)

One of the most talented anatomists of his time, he laid the foundation for paleontology as a science. Ideas he developed and tested were revolutionary in his day. These include anatomy studies that compare animal shapes and an "age of reptiles." His most radical idea was the discovery of extinction. Now these concepts form the basic makeup of biological study. He also named many species, including Pterodactylus and Mosasaurus.

Mary Anning (1799–1847)

Have you ever heard the tongue twister, "She Sells Seashells by the Sea Shore"? Mary Anning, an avid fossil hunter, inspired this little ditty. She and her family supported themselves by finding, repairing, and selling fossils. She discovered the first plesiosaur, one of the first ichthyosaurs, and even helped describe fossil poop! Her experience fossil hunting and keen mind won the respect of Europe's scientists. She worked with Georges Cuvier.

Joseph Leidy (1823–1891)

During the early days of paleontology, people viewed it as a hobby for the well-to-do. Joseph Leidy was a medical doctor. He innovated both in his professional field and in his fossil "hobby." He discovered that raw meat can hide parasites. He was also the first person to use a microscope to solve a murder mystery! On the fossil side, he named several species of Ice Age mammals, like dire wolves and the American lion. He described a Hadrosaurus, one of the first dinosaurs discovered in the US. His career shows how different scientific studies can work together to teach us about our world.

José Bonaparte (1928–2020)

When he was a kid, José and some friends started their own fossil museum in their hometown in Argentina. Since then, his efforts have drawn worldwide attention to Argentina. Now, scientists consider it one of the most important countries for fossil exploration. During his long career, he named sixty-four species of fossil animals. They range from the tiny Mussaurus baby dinosaurs to the gigantic Argentinosaurus. He also named the bizarre pterosaur Pterodaustro.

Halszka Osmólska (1930–2008)

A Polish paleontologist, she started her career studying trilobites. Later, she studied Mongolian dinosaurs, including the famous Velociraptor. Her studies explored how the body shapes of animals might have helped them survive. Her ideas gained international influence through publications and books such as *The Dinosauria*. In 2017, scientists named a strange swimming raptor-type dinosaur called a Halszkaraptor after her.

Dianne Edwards (1942–)

A paleobotanist is a paleontologist who studies plants. Paleobotanist Dianne Edwards happens to study the oldest fossil plants known. Her work has helped scientists understand how water plants adapted to harsh land environments. She has also served as President of the Linnean Society. It is the oldest organization in the world devoted to the science of studying living things.

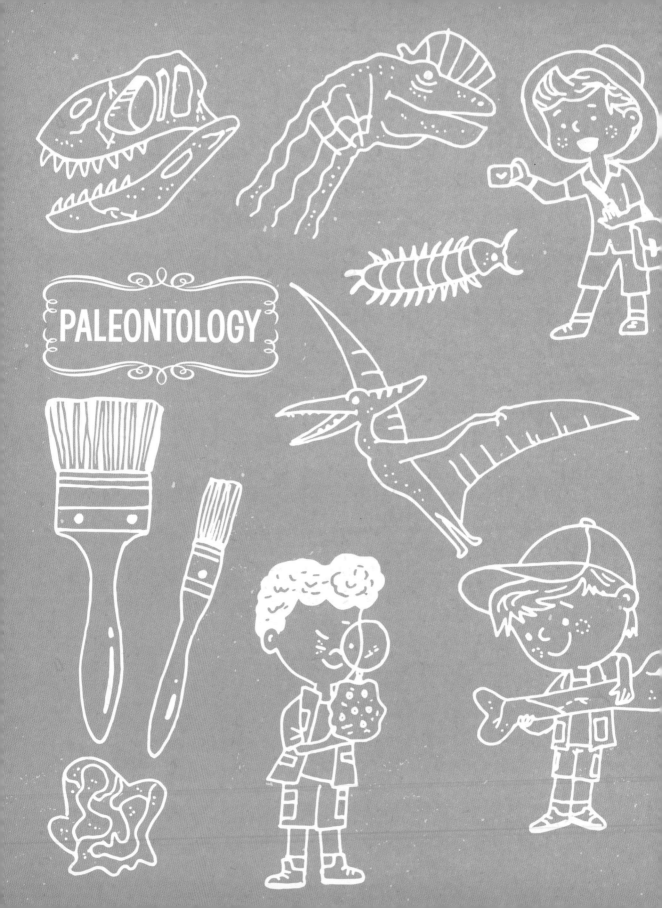

PALEONTOLOGY